ANECDOTES, FUN FACTS & FASCINATING HISTORY

By Kathy Heshelow
Sublime Beauty Naturals®
Member, NAHA

Anecdotes, Fun Facts & Fascinating History 2nd edition.
Essential Oils Have Super Powers® Series #2.

Text copyright ® 2016-2017 by Kathy Heshelow

This book is part of the original book Essential Oils Have Super Powers®: From Solving Everyday Wellness Problems to Taking on Superbugs.

ISBN 978-1-5210-8241-6 (book)
ALL RIGHTS RESERVED

No part of this publication may be reproduced, stored in a retrieval system, or transmitted in any form or by any means without the prior written consent of the publisher. Call 1-866-891-1031

Published by Sublime Beauty Naturals®
11125 Park Blvd, Suite 104-103, Seminole FL 33772
ISBN 978-1-4951-9496-2 (book) - ISBN 978-0-692-65198-8 (ebook)

Heshelow portrait by Heidi Haponowitz Photography

Printed in the United States

REVIEWS & WHAT PEOPLE ARE SAYING…

The author is clearly a true believer in the power of essential oils, and by the book's end, even skeptical readers may be tempted to give them a try. ~ Kirkus Reviews

…I especially liked the section where she goes into the history of essential oil throughout the centuries. There was ton of documented case studies and references should you want to get into it further. It truly is amazing the super powers these oils have. I strongly recommend the book…
~ Amazon Review, Deborah M.

Essential oils, whose benefits have been largely ignored by doctors in the U.S., offer a path to better health, according to this guide. Heshelow (Phytoceramides: Anti-Aging at Its Best, 2014, etc.) makes the case for aromatherapy and essential oils in this examination of a misunderstood branch of alternative medicine. ~ Kirkus Reviews

After Exploring the Wonders in This Book, You Might Want to Try Some Essential Oils For Yourself.

GET **FREE SAFETY TIPS FOR ESSENTIAL OILS + 50% OFF YOUR FIRST PURCHASE OF ESSENTIAL OILS** + other essential oil information & my next book free!

Visit:
https://goo.gl/x6SMQ7

Preface

My original book (Essential Oils Have Super Powers: From Solving Everyday Wellness Problems to Taking on Superbugs) encompasses many subjects about essential oils, and is rather long at 355 pages. While readers enjoy it, I also found that many today would love to read (or listen to) <u>shorter versions or specific chapters of interest</u>.

And so, I have created the "Essential Oils Have Super Powers® Series – this is #2, focusing on the fascinating history through the ages.

I feel so strongly about the valuable powers of essential oils that I trademarked the phrase: Essential Oils have Super Powers®. Some might be curious about this phrase, others might think it is hyperbole and roll their eyes. Those in the know will shake their head in agreement right away. My reasoning will become clear as you read through the fun facts, anecdotes and history.

You will be amazed how essential oils and aromatic plants have been used through history! It's a fun discover.

Now, if you are more interested in the antibacterial angle – the superbugs and how essential oils can seriously help – then pick up #1 in the series.

If you are more interested in knowing what essential oils are all about, and how you can use them in your everyday life (with recipes), then pick up series #3; if you are more interested in the Mind-Body-Spirit and Aromatherapy angle, then be sure to get series #4. And if you want the whole shebang (10 Chapters, 355 pages) in one book, then pick up the book!

My statement about essential oils? They awaken our senses; they can help with such conditions as depression, memory loss, sleeplessness, pain, focus, memory and anxiety. They can help improve our immune system. They can help create a tranquil environment, or one with energy. They can help with inflammation or specific injury healing (such as cuts, burns and bites). They can kill bacteria and microbes, cleanse our homes naturally, and so much more. This is why, to me, they have super powers!

Enjoy!

~ Kathy Heshelow
www.BooksByHeshelow.com | www.SublimeNaturals.com

TABLE OF CONTENTS

13 FUN FACTS TO START

CHAPTER 1

THE "OLDEST OF TIMES", VIBRANT SUMERIA THROUGH ANCIENT EGYPT INCLUDING THE PHARAOHS & CLEOPATRA!

CHAPTER 2

AYURVEDIC INDIA, ANCIENT CHINA, GREECE & ROME: HIPPOCRATES & NERO

CHAPTER 3

BIBLICAL TIMES TO EARLY PERSIA; MOSES & THE WISE MEN TO AVICENNA

CHAPTER 4

MEDIEVAL TIMES TO THE RENAISSANCE IN WESTERN EUROPE (1300-1700); MARCO POLO, THE PLAGUE & HENRI VIII

CHAPTER 4

MORE MODERN TIMES

REFERENCES

ACKNOWLEDGEMENTS

BIBLIOGRAPHY

13 FUN FACTS TO START

Fun Fact 1) Princess Di, Queen Victoria, Queen Elizabeth 1 and her father Henri VIII were all fans of aromatic plants and essential oils. It is said that Queen Elizabeth I and Queen truly loved lavender and used large amounts of it often. Henry VIII actually established a charter in 1543 proclaiming the right of herbalists to practice.

Fun Fact 2) The Catholic Church banned use of aromatherapy in the Dark Ages Europe because they did not like natural remedies and believed only God could cure maladies. (OK maybe this is not "fun" but it is a fact.)

Fun Fact 3) Ancient Greek warriors would not go into battle without myrrh (to help if they were injured.)

Fun Fact 4) Both Cleopatra and the Queen of Sheba liked to seduce lovers, it is said, with aromatic plants and oils, including lavender and rose.

Fun Fact 5) Hippocrates saved the day – and Athens

– by burning and diffusing aromatic plants to rid it of the plague.

Fun Fact 6) The Babylonians imported about 57,000 pounds of frankincense per year from Africa. This is back in 300 BC to 600 BC.

Fun Fact 7) It is reported that one of the earliest uses of the camel for business was for transporting frankincense and myrrh in trade!

Fun Fact 8) Shakespeare wrote in Hamlet, "There's rosemary, that's for remembrance", acknowledging its power on memory and focus, proven by researchers today.

Fun Fact 9) Magellan's ship (in 1522) returned to Spain loaded with Clove, to the delight of Spain.

Fun Fact 10) In 1855, the French sent eucalyptus plants to malaria-ridden areas of Algeria, and these area became malaria-free, dry zones. (This is thanks to two German botanist's suggestion that eucalyptus could be antiseptic.)

Fun Fact 11) Tea tree is Australia's oldest medicine! The aborigines have used it for centuries to treat infections, burns and wounds. This essential oil actually got its name courtesy Captain James Cook. He was in Australia and loved to brew the leaves for tea – the locals then named it "tea tree".

Fun Fact 12) During World War I, the British garden designer Gertrude Jekyll set aside a large plot of land just for the growing of marigolds (Calendula), which was shipped to France to treat burns victims.

Fun Fact 13) Peppermint has quite the history. Dried peppermint leaves were found in several Egyptian pyramids carbon dating back to 1,000 BC. Peppermint leaves were used in the Middle Ages to combat halitosis and whiten teeth.

CHAPTER 1 -

THE "OLDEST OF TIMES", VIBRANT SUMERIA THROUGH ANCIENT EGYPT INCLUDING THE PHARAOHS & CLEOPATRA!

Only the educated are free.
~Epictetus (55-135 A.D.)

Aromatic plants and essential oils have been used for thousands and thousands of years. People have long valued fragrances for their spiritual and physical cleansing, and pleasurable effects plus health applications.

I love history and understanding how things came to be or were developed over time. (My Bachelor's degree was in art history in Paris, which pulled together art, politics, religion, science, economics and lifestyles of each era.) When I started studying the history of essential oils, I typically found a paragraph to a page stating that essential oils were first used in

Ancient Egypt; mention of Ancient Greece and Rome; and then zoom forward to the early 1900's and René-Maurice Gattefossé, considered the father of "modern" aromatherapy – he coined the term and devoted his life to its study in the south of France.

I wanted to go deeper into the history of essential oils, and indeed found really interesting facts to share with you! So here we go!

The first thing to state: essential oils as we use them today were not as such until steam distillation was "invented". Susruta, an Ayurvedic master in the 2nd century, described in the Book of Ayurveda how to obtain rose oil, citronella oil and calamus by distillation.(1) Ancient Egyptians were familiar with fire and the distillation process, producing turpentine, for instance.

There is evidence of crude distillation apparati at several archaeological sites and in a few museums (Cyprus, Iraq, the area that is now Syria and elsewhere) dating prior to ancient Egypt. Aromatic plants and infused waters or the aromatic essences in fat-soluble solutions were certainly used with beneficial results.

However, the first more modern <u>documented</u> proof of steam distillation machinery came with the brilliant Avicenna (10th century) – you'll read more about him in this chapter. So, while frankincense, peppermint and myrrh are valued just as much today as they were centuries ago when mentioned in various texts, they were just in a slightly different "format" than in our more modern era.

THE BEGINNINGS

The roots and history of aromatherapy is believed to have begun with the burning of fragrant woods, leaves, needles, and tree gums. The first evidence of early humans using fire dates back to more than a million years, but the practice did not become routine until about

650,000 years later.

This practice of burning fragrant plants probably arose once it was discovered that when burning certain plants, such as cypress and cedar, scents filled the air and perhaps some change of mood or even wellness effects were felt or discovered. (Of course, this is speculation on my part but it seems logical.)

We do know that plants were viewed as powerful, considered to have magical attributes and were employed in various ceremonies, applications and healing rituals to appease the spirits and combat curses (2)

CAVES IN THE SOUTH OF FRANCE

The earliest evidence of human knowledge of the healing properties of plants was found in Lascaux, located in the Dordogne region in France (France again!). There, cave paintings suggest the use of medicinal plants in everyday life that have been carbon dated as far back as 18,000 B.C.

The archeological evidence for medicinal use of plants (including oils) by humans in the areas that are now Texas and northeastern Mexico extends back 10,500 years ago. Psychoactive plants have a long history of use in the form of smoke for ritual and medicinal purposes - the early precursors of aromatherapy. In many cultures, plant smoke is still widely used in cleansing rituals and is believed to carry messages to the spirit world. That very same belief is behind the burning of frankincense in Catholic churches.

SUMERIA & BABYLON

Ancient written records (clay tablets) documenting the medicinal use of plants come to us from the ancient Sumerians, who lived in Mesopotamia from about 5,500 B.C. Sumeria is often referred to as the cradle of civilization (along with Akkad and Babylon). Aromatic essences were quite highly prized with the Sumerians. The written records actually detail what they used, how they prepared the plants or oils and dosages.

Sumerian clay tablet

In Sumeria, clay pots were filled with plant material which was then covered in water; an absorbent cloth of some kind was stuffed into the opening and the pot heated. As the water turned to steam and rose towards the opening of the jar, the essential oils were trapped in the material, which could then be wrung out to produce a mixture of water and essential oils that would have been similar to today's hydrosols.

Myrrh is mentioned in one of the oldest epics, the Gilgamesh from Mesopotamia, in which Ut-napitschti, the urfather thanks God for his salvation from the

Deluge by burning cedarwood and myrrh.

The Babylonians, who lived in the same general area from about 3000 B.C. to 600 B.C. also left records detailing the use of medicinal herbs and plants. The Assyrians followed the Babylonians in about 628 B.C. They not only preserved the clay tablets of the earlier civilizations, but left their own. They believed that disease was largely considered to be the work of evil spirits or demons (a belief that passed through many eras). The most common way of ridding themselves of these demons was smoking them out with fragrant plants. Mentioned in the various texts were chamomile, myrrh, turmeric and calendula.

I found it exciting that there was an enormous trade in aromatic plants in the ancient world. <u>The Babylonians imported frankincense from Africa and burned about 57,000 pounds of it a year. The Assyrians burned about 120,000 pounds of it a year in their annual feast of Baal.</u> In fact, Babylon became the center of the aromatics trade in the late 5th century B.C. and among the most common plants they used were cypress, pine, fir, myrtle, frankincense, calamus and juniper.

ANCIENT EGYPTIANS

The Egyptians are probably most famous for their use of aromatic plants and oils. They made extensive use of resins, dried plants, infused oils and pomades. Fragrant plants were used for embalming, for religious rituals, for diffusing in living spaces and for healing; it is known they commonly used cedar, myrrh, and frankincense among others.

The earliest historical accounts of the Egyptian use of aromatics date to about 4,500 B.C. - about 1000 years <u>after</u> the Sumerians. However, the most famous historical document describing the use of aromatic medicine by the Egyptians is the Ebers Papyrus, (found near Thebes in 1872.) The Ebers Papyrus was written during the reign of Khufu, around 2800 B.C., and describes the use of over <u>850 botanical remedies</u> including myrrh, frankincense, myrtle, galbanum and many other aromatic herbs. The use of myrrh as a wound salve is mentioned specifically.

Gattefossé wrote in his book that embalming dates back beyond ancient Egypt (they just perfected it) to the Copper Age or beginning of the Bronze Age. (3). He further wrote that many ancient rites used essential oils or spices, burned in their natural state (like juniper, rosemary). The aromatics created an emotional atmosphere but the holy sites like temples were seen as very healthy and pure, too. The essential oils or aromatic plants were of course overcoming microbes and bacteria.

Ancient Egyptians used incense, essential oils, infused waters, ointments and resins for various religious ceremonies. The anti-bacterial and anti-microbial properties of essential oils or their plant material was very important in the embalming process!

Egyptians used frankincense on a large scale, burning it for purification in sacred spaces and for use in the pharaoh's living spaces. It is said that terra cotta urns filled with aromatic essential oils accompanied the pharaohs to the afterlife. Oils of cedarwood, clove, cinnamon, nutmeg and myrrh were used to embalm the dead (discovered in some tombs that were opened in this century. It was reported that some light scents of various oils remained at discovery!)

King Tutankhamun was entombed with roughly 350 liters of aromatic oil including cedarwood, frankincense, and myrrh.

In 1370 BC, Pharoah Amenophis IV (later known as Akhenaten), husband of Nefertiti, received a request from Milkili, one of his military lieutenants serving in Palestine saying, "And let the King, my Lord, send troops to his servants, and let the King, my Lord, send myrrh for medicine." It was said that he refused to fight until the physicians with his troops had a good supply of myrrh . (4)

In art history classes, I loved learning that Egyptian men of the time used fragrance as much as the women. An interesting method used (seen in tomb art) was to place a solid cone of aromatic plants or perfume on their heads (as seen here). It would gradually melt and cover them in fragrance.

It is reported that Queen Hatshepsut's expedition to the legendary land of Punt (about 1470 B.C.) was a truly great adventure of antiquity. Her army brought back wondrous riches - the greatest of all the treasures was a grove of myrrh trees. Punt is said to be modern-day Somalia.

Queen Cleopatra kept massive gardens of hundreds of flowers and used their essences to perfume her body and surroundings. Both the Queen of Sheba and Cleopatra loved lavender and rose for various purposes (including seducing lovers, it is said!)

By 500 B.C. the Nile Valley was considered the

'Cradle of Medicine' because of its expert use of oils and herbs for healing.

In fact, Egyptian medicine went hand in hand with religion, thought and mind. The use of aromatic plants and natural oils was originally used only by the Pharaohs and priests. The priests and "clergy" eventually developed pharmacies for healing which was quite sophisticated.

CHAPTER 2

AYURVEDIC INDIA, ANCIENT CHINA, GREECE & ROME: HIPPOCRATES & NERO

During the time when Egyptians were using plants and oils for perfumes, incense, and embalming, early healers in India developed the Ayurvedic system of medicine - the oldest form of medicine.

Ayurveda is from ayur "life" + veda "knowledge" and is based on the idea of balance in bodily systems and uses diet, herbal treatment, and yogic breathing.
"Ayurvedic practices include the use of herbal medicines, mineral or metal supplementation (rasa shastra), surgical techniques, opium, and application of oil by massages." (5)

A portion of the Rig Veda written around 4,500 BC records the use of aromatic herbs. As mentioned at the beginning of the Chapter, the Book of Ayurveda and Susruta included information about essential oil use and its application in the 2nd century.

CHINA

Legendary Chinese ruler Shen Nung is credited with discovering the medicinal properties of plants and writing the first herbal text, 'Pen Tsao' (c. 2700-3000 B.C.), which is a catalog of more than 200 botanicals.

The first herbal of Chinese medicine, written in the second century, also known as Shen Nung Ben Cao, classifies plants in the categories of prevention, restorative and treatment. It addresses the jing (essence) of plants, corresponding to our understanding of essential oils. The Chinese 'Yellow Emperor's Classic of Internal Medicine', was written in 2697 B.C. and is the oldest surviving medical book in China.

ANCIENT GREECE AND ROME

The ancient Greeks used an array of essential oils. We know they used lavender to fight insomnia, insanity and some pains like back aches. Greek soldiers carried myrrh into battle with them to use for skin infections, cuts and gangrene.

After Alexander's invasion of Egypt in the 3rd century B.C., the use of aromatics, herbs and perfumes became much more popular in Greece prompting great interest in all things aromatic!

The wonderful Greek physician Hippocrates (460 to 375 B.C.) is considered the father of modern medicine. It is said that he used essential oils for baths and purification for medicinal purposes. Historical records showed he fumigated Athens with plant aromatics saving many from a plague.

Hippocrates wrote "a perfumed bath and a scented massage every day is the way to good health." He believed in natural substances for health, and also wrote; "Above all the purpose of a doctor is to awaken the natural healing energies within the body".

Theophrastus of Athens, who was a philosopher and student of Aristotle, investigated everything about plants and <u>even how scents affected the emotions</u>. He wrote several volumes on botany including 'The History of Plants', which became a top botanical science reference for centuries to come. He is generally referred to today as the "Founder of Botany".

Between 300 B.C. and 100 B.C. Persian traders brought myrrh and frankincense from Yemen to the Mediterranean, especially Greece and Rome, and soon demand grew for roses, saffron, spikenard, ginger and many other aromatics. The first century AD was a time of great progress for aromatherapy. About 2,800 tons of Frankincense was imported to Rome per year during this era, and Pliny's book, "Natural History", includes 32 flower remedies. (6)

A Greek perfumer by the name of Megallus created a perfume called "megaleion" which became quite popular and well-used. Megaleion included myrrh in a fatty-oil base and served several purposes: (a) as a perfume, (b) as an anti-inflammatory remedy for the skin and (c) as a product to heal wounds. It included myrrh and cinnamon.

Pliny the Elder (23-79 A.D.) described a widely used essential oil blend called kyphi (some references to it may go back to Egyptian times.) It included cypress, juniper, frankincense, myrrh, calamus and other aromatics mixed with honey. Kyphi was used for medical purposes and in worship. Dioscordes wrote that kyphi brought relaxation, promoted sleep and calm. The Roman historian and botanist Pliny the Elder also recommended frankincense as an antidote to hemlock poisoning, and wrote in the first century A.D. that this amazing resin had made the southern Arabians the richest people on earth.

Pedanius Dioscordes (30-90 A.D.) had a passion for plants, and catalogued all the known herbs and their uses in his enormous work, "De Materia Medica" (five volumes) in 70 A.D. Dioscordes was born in Turkey and became a traveling physician, even traveling with Nero's army. Most of his works were written in Greek, and they became known by many, and then translated into many languages.

To make a comparison as far as the depth of what Dioscordes did: everything Hippocrates wrote on medicinal plants totals about 130 articles. Dioscordes listed over 4,740 different uses in his book, and lists more than 360 varieties of medicinal actions.

He took a very scientific approach: Dioscorides didn't accept anything on faith or "hear-say", or on the reputation of established authorities; he checked everything out himself that he included in his books, and tested every drug clinically. He personally traveled and researched the local folk medicine uses of every herb he wrote about.

Another brilliant Greek physician was Claudius Galen, who lived from 129-199 A.D. and studied medicine from the age of seventeen. He began his medical career at age 28 under the Romans, treating wounds of gladiators with medicinal herbs - and it is said that not a single gladiator died of battle wounds while under his care.

Roman soldiers treated wounds with honey and

myrrh, while emperors and scholars relaxed in legendary perfumed baths. Romans loved using lavender in the public baths. In both Greece and Rome, Myrrh was used as a remedy for skin sores, for treating mouth and eye infections, as a cough remedy, against worm infestation and even for cattle abdominal pains.

Due to his phenomenal success, Galen quickly rose to become the personal physician to the Roman Emperor, Marcus Aurelius, and since Rome was a thriving academic center during his lifetime, it was the ideal place to conduct further research. Galen was the last of the great Greco-Roman physicians, and within 100 years of his death the Roman Empire would begin to decline, plunging Europe into the dark ages.

Suzanne Bovenizer CMT, CST, writes about the Romans (7):

> *The Romans took the use of essential oils to new extremes. In self-indulgent Rome, lavish baths were created as focal points for Roman life. Men would gather in the mid afternoon at these communal bathing facilities and not only soak in water, but compete in sports like wrestling, have business*

meetings, wander through gardens and enjoy entertainment. Before the sports, men would be oiled up usually with olive oil, then have their bodies scraped with a curved metal wire to take off excess dirt and sweat. Plunges into a variety of bathes from cool to hot were followed with massages rich in fragrant unguents.

There were 3 main types of perfumes used at this time: "Ladysmata" were solid unguents, "Stymmata" were scented oils, and "Diapasmata" were powdered perfumes. Recipes for favorite aromatics used during this period were archived. One was called "Susinum" which was a combination of honey, calamus, cinnamon, myrrh, and saffron. "Nardinum" brought together calamus, costus, cardamom, melissa, spikenard and myrrh. These would be used in cosmetics, or in massage, rubbed on hair, or even scented bed clothes. One interesting note was that the scent of orange was reserved only for courtesans and ladies of a similar trade, which if you think of the aphrodisiac qualities of neroli, you can imagine why… As stated earlier, men enjoyed smelling as sweetly as women. Although women were allowed to use the bathes, they had to pay more and usually met only in the mornings, staying segregated from the men. By 3 AD, Rome was the bathing capital of Europe, with 1,000 fragrant spas in the city alone. Nero, the then debauched, self-serving emperor, lavished himself in scented bliss, particularly taking pleasure in the scent of roses, believing that the oil not only uplifted spirits, but also helped with headaches and indigestion. One would drink out of perfumed cups and walk through spice-scented rooms when visiting Nero's palace. Unguents were being so widely used by that point in history, that in 30 AD supplies of exotic plants and herbs were becoming scarce. An edict was drafted encouraging less personal use of aromatics so that the supplies could be used more for medicinal, religious and ritual purposes.(7)

CHAPTER 3

BIBLICAL TIMES TO EARLY PERSIA; MOSES & THE WISE MEN TO AVICENNA

Around 1200 B.C., the Book of Exodus records how the Jews took too much knowledge of herbs and spices with them as they fled from Egypt. A recipe for an anointing oil was given to Moses (blending myrrh, cinnamon, calamus and olive oils 500-400 B.C.)

The Old and New Testaments of the Bible contain recipes using aromatic compounds – there are more than 500 references to Essential Oils (especially frankincense and myrrh, cedarwood and spikenard, which is part of the valerian family.)

The wise men, as we know, brought the valuable gift of frankincense and myrrh to the birth of Jesus – they were considered as valuable as gold. Mary used lavender to anoint Jesus' feet.

According to David Stewart (Healing Oils of the Bible), the "Rose of Sharon" in the Song of Soloman is thought to be ladanum, also called Rock Rose.

Frankincense and myrrh are mentioned the most, according to Stewart, and it is not surprising. They are analgesics with other medicinal powers, so very helpful. Spikenard, hyssop, workwood and cedarwood the next most frequent, followed by myrtle, the aloes, cypress and cinnamon.

Aromatic oils were used for anointing, for oinments and salves, for joy and for worship.

THRIVING EARLY PERSIA

Al-Razi (865-925) is considered one of Persia's finest physicians. Like many intellectuals in his day, he lived at various small courts under the patronage of minor rulers. During his lifetime he wrote more than 237 books and articles covering several fields of science, half of which concerned medicine. Quite a few were translated into Latin. Born in the town of Rayy near Tehran, Al-Razi was known in the West as Rhazes where he had great influence on European science and medicine.

His most influential work was a medical encyclopedia covering 25 books called "Al Kitab al Hawi", which was later translated into Latin and other European languages, and known in English as "The Comprehensive Work".

His medical accomplishments were legendary. This man was quite amazing - he developed such things as spatulas, mortars, and flasks used in pharmacies for centuries (until the 1900s).

In the 10th century, the well-known Persian philosopher, child genius, physician and scientist Avicenna (980 to 1037) "invented" and used the first steam distillation for essential oils, later refined during the Renaissance in western Europe. Avicenna invented a coiled pipe which allowed the plant vapor and steam to cool down more effectively than previous distillers that used a straight cooling pipe. Avicenna's contribution led to more focus on essential oils and their benefits in the years that followed.

At the age of 16 Avicenna began studying medicine and by 20 he had been appointed a court physician, earning the title 'Prince of Physicians'. He wrote books covering theology, metaphysics, astronomy, philology, philosophy and poetry, and most influentially, 20 books and 100 treatises on medicine.

His 14 volume epic "Al-Qanun fi al-Tibb", which means "The Canon of Medicine" was over one million words long. It included the total of what was known to that day of existing medical knowledge, including Galen and Hippocrates and other eminent figures who preceded him.

Anecdote: when the sultan of Bukhara became ill and the court physicians couldn't figure it out or help him, Avicenna was called to his bedside - and cured him! This earned him the gratitude of the sultan, who opened the royal Sāmānid library to him. This was an amazing gift, giving him access to much knowledge and written works on medicine and science.

Another anecdote: Avicenna excelled at the preparation of rose water (a favored plant of Persians) and other infused oil waters by blowing live steam into the distillation vessel filled with plants. Thus, it seems relatively certain that Avicenna invented the more modern process of steam distillation.

CHAPTER 4

MEDIEVAL TIMES TO THE RENAISSANCE IN WESTERN EUROPE (1300-1700); MARCO POLO, THE PLAGUE & HENRI VIII

As the Romans began pulling out of Britain and Europe, much of their vast medical knowledge that had been collected and passed from Greece, ancient Egypt, Persia and other enlightened places was all but discarded. All progress in the Western tradition of medicine came to a halt for hundreds of years, in a time appropriately nicknamed "The Dark Ages."

In fact, after the fall of the Roman Empire, the use of aromatic plants waned as Europe fell backwards into this unfortunate period. To escape disaster, many physicians and the educated relocated to Constantinople (which is Istanbul today), and along with them went so much knowledge, to safeguard and survive. As European civilization stumbled, the educated translated the works of Hippocrates, Dioscorides, and others mentioned here, widely distributing them in the Middle East.

The oldest surviving English manuscript of botanical medicine is the Saxon "Leech Book of Bald", which was written between 900 and 950 by a scribe named Cild under the direction of Bald, who was a friend of King Alfred the Great. ("Leech" is an old English word meaning healer). This book includes descriptions of 500 plants and how they could be used internally or externally. In addition to herbalism, it includes magic, shamanism and ceremonial rites.

Interestingly, as recently reported by the BBC (March 2015) on antibiotic resistant bacteria, the "Leech Book of Bald" and a specific recipe were cited:

"Scientists recreated a 9th Century Anglo-Saxon remedy using onion, garlic and part of a cow's stomach. They were "astonished" to find it almost completely wiped out methicillin-resistant staphylococcus aureus, otherwise known as MRSA. Their findings will be presented at a national microbiology conference ...Anglo-Saxon expert Dr. Christina Lee, from the University of Nottingham, translated the recipe...Experts from the university's microbiology team recreated the remedy and then tested it on large cultures of MRSA ... In each case, they tested the individual ingredients against the bacteria, as well as the remedy and a control solution. They found the remedy killed up to 90% of MRSA bacteria and believe it is the effect of the recipe rather than one single ingredient." (8)

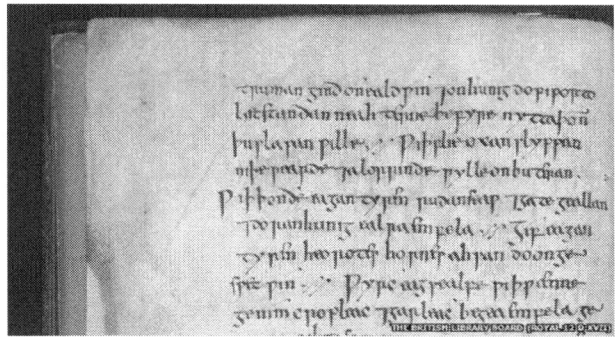

courtesy British Library: Leech Book of Bald

When the Crusaders returned from the Holy Wars (1095-1291), they brought with them aromatic plants, perfumes and healing remedies that were previously unknown or had been discarded centuries prior. Fragrant plants became increasingly popular, with aromatic herb garlands decorating homes and rose water being used to wash the hands of those who could afford it. The availability and range of aromatic medicines continued to increase over the next few hundred years.

Frankincense and myrrh became popular after being discovered through the returning Crusaders. However, they were so expensive that the area which traded and imported it, southern Arabia, became known as Arabia Felix, "Arabia the Blessed."

An early description of distillation in Europe is from the Catalan physician Arnald de Villanova (1235-1311) whom it is said introduced the art into early European therapy.

Marco Polo and Kubla Khan

With Marco Polo (1254-1324), the much-prized spices and aromatics of India, China, and beyond sparked European trade and renewed interest. Spices and oils such as cardamom, sage, cinnamon, and nutmeg were reintroduced, and pharmacists (such as they were in the era) began to work with the imports more.

In the 12th century, Hildegard, an Abbess of Germany, is said to have grown and distilled lavender for its medicinal properties. The iconic Cathedral in Santiago de Compostelo (Spain), where pilgrimages were led year after year since Medieval times (think "Canterbury Tales"), has the largest Frankincense burner in the world.

The "Red Book of Hergest" is a large vellum manuscript written shortly after 1382 in Wales. It ranks as one of the most important medieval manuscripts written in the Welsh language. Not only is there poetry and historical stories, but it also includes herbal remedies. These were associated with Rhiwallon Feddyg, founder of a medical dynasty in Wales that lasted over 500 years. 'The Physicians of Myddfai were from the village of Myddfai - this text is being reexamined again today for secrets and research into essential oils.

The horrid Black Death appeared in the 14th century (around 1347), killing millions of people across Europe. It was devastating. Almost 50% of London's inhabitants succumbed within the first year, and up to 40% of the entire population of Europe would die within 3 years.

In Europe at that time, medicine was almost entirely governed by the Catholic Church. The church considered illness and disease to be a punishment from God or even demons incarnate, and the standard form of treatment administered by the priests was prayer, and perhaps a session of blood-letting. The Church rejected "pagan fragrances" because they stimulated forbidden instincts or heightened pleasure. The church saw physicians and their plants and oils as competition for curing mind and soul as well as unreligious. Sigh.

Historical anecdote: During the plague in France (around 1400 A.D.), four thieves in Marseilles were robbing the unfortunate dead – without becoming sick. When they were eventually caught, their secret was revealed: they used a blend of essential oils and aromatics to protect themselves from getting sick. The blend included cinnamon, rosemary, clove, eucalyptus and lemon. Today, there are essential oil blends called Thieves or Four Thieves, in memory of the event.

In fact, during this period perfumers and tanners in England and France escaped the Plague, too, due to the overwhelming amounts of aromatic plans and essential oils they used which passed on the antibacterial qualities.

Moufitte, a writer during the period, noted in his book "Treatise on Food" that an entire town in England called Bucklersbury was "replete" with spices and oils. Being so perfumed in the time of the plague, it escaped as multitudes died in the next towns away. In Shakespeare's "The Merry Wives of Windsor", Falstaff makes a reference to the aromatic Bucklersbury: "Come, I cannot cog, and say thou art this and that like many of these lisping hawthorn buds, that come like women in men's apparel, and smell like Bucklersbury in simple time." Bucklersbury was the center of the European Lavender trade.

Despite the Church forbidding aromatic oils, herbal preparations were used to help fight this terrible killer. It is believed that some perfumers and herbalists may have avoided the plague due to their continual contact with essential oils and plants (with anti-bacterial and cleansing power.)

Certainly, when the Black Death made its second appearance in 1603, virtually every available aromatic was burned in houses and on the streets to help keep the plaque at bay. Benzoin, frankincense and various spice oils were all used to prevent the spread of this deadly disease. The only people not to succumb in large numbers to the plague (both times) were the workers involved in aromatics and perfumery, and this is undoubtedly due to the highly antiseptic properties of the essential oils.

RENAISSANCE

The Renaissance revitalized everything in European society, including aromatherapy with imports from the East; explorer merchants brought back exotic herbs and oils. With the Renaissance and certainly by the 15th century, things were evolving more quickly. More plants were distilled to create essential oils including frankincense, juniper, rose, sage and rosemary. A growth in the amount of books on herbs and their properties also begins later in the century.

Herbal medicine was used by all, from peasants to kings. King Henry VIII (born 1491) was a huge advocate of herbal medicine and as well as treatment from his own apothecaries, even enjoyed making his own remedies. His charter of 1543 gave herbalists the right to practice (although it was taken away later). Records show that Tudors in Henry VIII's time treated headaches by drinking a mixture of lavender, sage, marjoram, rose and rue, as just one example.

Paracelsus (1493-1541) was an alchemist, author, teacher, medical doctor and philosopher born near Zurich. He is credited with coining the term "Essence" or "quinta essential" for essential oils. His studies radically challenged the nature of alchemy as he focused upon using plants as medicines. He moved away from the medical applications of his day which included bleeding and purging; he travelled widely and gathered information. However, he incurred the wrath of many with his eccentric character, and by rejecting Galen and Avicenna. (9)

In 1564, the authors Charles Estienne and Jean Liebaul wrote in L'Agriculture et Maison Rustique: "Distilled oils are found by experience to be more valid, more efficacious, more pleasant, and of more rapid effect than any other, to cure all kinds of difficult diseases, especially wounds, ulcers…" (10)

Of note, around this time (about 1500 A.D.), Spanish Conquistadors invaded the Aztecs, and were amazed to find an abundance of aromatic, medicinal herbs in Montezuma's garden and knowledge of its use.

Queen Elizabeth I (1533-1603), the daughter of Henri VIII, used an abundant supply of English lavender oil throughout her life, a practice continued by Queen Victoria during her entire 64-year reign. (The tradition was upheld in the 20th century by Diana, Princess of Wales, who regularly visited her aromatherapist. It is known that her living quarters were usually fragrant with various essential oils.)

A German physician, Hieronymus Braunschweig, wrote several books on essential oil distillation which went through hundreds of editions in every European language at the time. In 1597 he referenced 25 essential oils included rosemary, lavender, clove, cinnamon, myrrh, and nutmeg.

Many books about distillation of essential oils were written in the 16th century, especially in Germany, which seemed to be one of the centers of an aromatherapy renaissance.

Several English sources from the 1500s and 1600s give detailed recipes for sweet waters and for distilling essential oils, such as Gervase Markham's 1615 "English Housewife", John French's 1653 "Art of Distillation", and Hugh Plat's 1594 "Delightes for Ladies". Many (modern or contemporary) sources claim that the oldest alcohol based perfumes were

Queen of Hungary Water (a rosemary-based water) and Carmelite water (or King Charles' water), whose ingredients vary-- both allegedly "invented" in the late 1300s and originally used as medicinal doses and rubs.

During the 16th century, one could buy oils at an "apothecary," and many more essential oils were introduced, thanks to growing trade and interested populace. This widespread use of essential oils throughout Europe coincided with the invention of glass distillation methods in the 16th century, the discovery of new trade routes east and the invention of the microscope, which facilitated the study of bio-active compounds.

And in fact, in the 16th century, there were comprehensive plant catalogs available. Anyone who could read had access to recipes for oils, perfumed waters and other methods of treating plants for wellness. Advancements in distillation techniques were made in Germany during the 16th century.

Shakespeare wrote in Hamlet (said by Orphelia):

"There's rosemary that's for remembrance", acknowledging the power of that essential oil or herb on memory and focus, proven out through researchers today.

Nicholas Culpepper (1616-1654) was one of the most influential herbalists of his time. In his most famous work, "The English Physician" (1652), Culpeper's descriptions of herbs, oils and their uses were intermixed with astrology. It should be noted that in the 17th century, Nicholas Culpeper wrote passionate works against doctors who were using and prescribing poisonous substances such as mercury on patients. (11)

The first and earliest industrial essential oil manufacturers appear in Europe from 1768, according to "Handbook of Essential Oils: Science, Technology, and Applications" edited by K. Husnu Can Baser and Gerhard Buchbauer. These early manufacturers include:

Antoine Chiris (1768) in Grasse, France; Cavallier Freres (1784) in Grasse, France; Dodge & Alcott

(1798) in New York (*listed as importers*); Roure Bertrand Fils et Justin Dupont (1820) in Grasse, France; Schimmel & Co (1829) in Leipzig, Germany; M. Mero-Boyveau (1832) in Grasse, France; Standford, Allen & Sons (1833) London; Robertet et Cie (1850) in Grasse, France; and W.J. Bush (1851) London.

Grasse in the south of France has always been an area of aromatic plants, lavender, perfumeries and such. For the New York importers, I tried to track down more information on Dodge & Alcott and didn't get far. They seemed to have favored importing perfumes.

CHAPTER 4

MORE MODERN TIMES

American companies began manufacturing products with essential oils, like soaps and perfumes. Most of this industry was located in New York, with its access to imported spices, aromatics and French fragrances. As far as essential oils, it seemed the emphasis was more on household products and synthetic products rather than a large-scale population recognizing them for healing, as in Europe and the East.

There were holistic, homeopath and naturopath movements during this time, of course, with some quite devoted to the new natural movements - and other "traditionalists" who were quite hostile to the movement.

Back in Europe, with the rise of chemistry in the late 19th century, the demystification developed and more availability essential oils developed thanks to the distillation process.

In 1867 a curious thing happened in the world of essential oils. (12) The official concept of "perfume for cosmetics" appeared at the Paris International Exhibition - "Exposition Universelle". For the first time perfumes, scented gloves, and soaps where clearly displayed <u>separately</u> from medicinal plant essences. The exposition began on April 1, 1867 and closed on October 31, 1867 with over 9,000,000 visitors! This seems to be the beginning of the division of scent for health vs scent just for the sake of scent without regards to health.

RENE-MAURICE GATTEFOSSE

Modern aromatherapy is memorialized and "born" with French chemist Rene-Maurice Gattefossé, who worked for a prominent perfumer in the south of France (Grasse). One day there was a horrible accident in the lab and he set his arm on fire. Contrary to what is found on many websites, Robert Tisserand confirms he DID NOT thrust his arm into the nearest vat of lavender oil willy-nilly. The translation of Gattefossé's own words by Tisserand:

> "The external application of small quantities of essences rapidly stops the spread of gangrenous sores. In my personal experience, after a laboratory explosion covered me with burning substances which I extinguished by rolling on a grassy lawn, both my hands were covered with a rapidly developing gas gangrene. Just one rinse with lavender essence stopped "the gasification of the tissue". This treatment was followed by profuse sweating, and healing began the next day (July 1910)." (13)

His application of lavender oil was clearly an <u>intentional</u> act, not accidental. However, because the results were very impressive, this is a very impactful moment for him and for the history of essential oils and aromatherapy. This was a serious burn and his life had been threatened (gas gangrene was potentially life-threatening.) In addition, previous chemical burns he had received had caused severe pain, redness, blisters and scarring. This bad burn healed with minimal pain and no scarring. And so this incident and discovery of the healing power of lavender began his interest, and then his commitment and lifelong work, with essential oils – to our benefit today!

As was mentioned previously, Gattefossé coined the word "aromatherapie" to describe the healing experience and work with essential oils. He spent the rest of his life researching health benefits of essential oils and collaborating with other doctors and scientists. In 1937, he published his findings and book "Aromatherapie" ("Aromatherapy"). It was translated into English in 1993 by Robert Tisserand and the 2nd edition is still in print, 70 years after it was written (I love my copy and refer to it even today). He is credited with the modern therapeutic approach to holistic healing and balance with essential oils.

French physician Jean Valnet took up and continued the work of Gattefossé during World War II, using chamomile, clove, lemon and thyme essential oils to successfully treat wounded soldiers with gangrene, greatly reducing the need for amputation. After graduating as a surgeon at the end of the war, Valnet continued to use essential oils to treat illnesses, and he was the first ever documented doctor to use them to treat psychiatric conditions. Dr. Valnet recognized the powerful anti-bacterial qualities of essential oils after numerous tests and experiments, and concluded, "Clearly, the administering of essential oils should be common practice in sick rooms, operating rooms and clinics." (14)

During World War II, all Australian soldiers were issued tea tree oil in their first aid kits. The troops used it as an insect repellent and for its fungal-fighting properties.

Historical anecdote stepping back a decade: With the advent of World War I, the demand for medicine was huge, due to the enormous number of casualties, and herbs were widely used. The garden designer, Gertrude Jekyll set aside a large plot of land just for the growing of Marigolds (Calendula), which was shipped to France to treat burns victims.

Then, during WWII, the British government appealed

to the public to help grow herbs for the war effort. In 1940, Whitechapel hospital alerted Kew Gardens that essential supplies of medicines were virtually depleted. Very quickly the Vegetable Drugs Committee was formed, made up of members of the Ministry of Agriculture and Fisheries, Kew, Pharmaceutical Society and herb growers. Lists of essential plants were drawn up and volunteers helped collect them (including school children and Scouts.) The plants were sold to botanical drug companies to make conventional medicines!

France and active French scientists who were working with essential oils had an influence on the U.K. in this regard.

Valnet's inspired book, 'Aromathérapie - Traitment des Maladies par les Essence de Plantes' (Aromatherapy – Treatment of Illnesses with Essential Oils) was released in 1964. It popularized aromatherapy for medical and psychiatric use throughout France in the 1960s The book was translated into English in 1980, published under the new title of 'The Practice of Aromatherapy', which put aromatherapy squarely on the English map.

Marguerite Maury (1895-1968) was an Austrian-born biochemist who became interested in essential oils, after reading a book written in 1838 by Dr. Chabenes called, "Les Grandes Possibilités par les Matières Odoriferantes". (Dr. Chabenes would become the teacher of Gattefossé.) She published her book in 1962 about the benefits of essential oils, "Le Capital Jeunesse" in France, but sadly did not initially receive the acclaim that it deserved. However, when it was released in Britain in 1964 under the title of "The Secret of Life and Youth", it finally gained recognition.

After her death, the work of Maury continued through her protege, Danièle Ryman, who today is now herself considered an authority on aromatherapy.

The first modern English language book, "The Art of Aromatherapy" by British citizen Robert Tisserand (1977), introduced the benefits of aromatherapy coupled with massage and advanced the practice in the United Kingdom and the United States. Tisserand is a giant in the field of aromatherapy today.

The work of Valnet and Gattefossé stimulated and influenced him. His book became the inspiration and reference for virtually every future author on the subject for almost two decades.

Dr. Paul Belaiche published a three-volume work on the clinical uses of aromatherapy for infectious and degenerative diseases in 1978.

Henri Viaud is also important to mention here in the modern history of aromatherapy. He is a master distiller and led the charge for pure non-unadulterated essential oils that are authentic. Some producers at this time would adulterate oils, but he was firm (and had the voice) that for therapeutic, medicinal value, essential oils must be genuine and pure as distilled.

I will also mention Dr. Kurt Schnaubelt here. He earned his Ph.D in Germany (Technical University of Munich), and has become a leader of aromatherapy in the United States since 1983. He is author of many books on the subject and scientific director of the Pacific Institute of Aromatherapy. He is quoted in this book several times, including on the next pages!

After WWII: Pharma Plus Chemicals

After World War II a huge increase was seen in the production of petrochemicals and synthetics. Production of these chemicals has increased greatly over the years. In 1940 petrochemicals and synthetics were produced at the rate of one billion pounds per year; compare that to 1980 over 400 billion pounds per year were produced (Steinman & Epstein, 1995). Since 1965 more than four million distinct chemical compounds have been reported in scientific literature and of these seventy thousand are used in commercial production. (15)

With the onset of this chemical production "boom", an increase in health problems has been observed such as asthma and allergies. Other conditions have been noted as well such as headaches, insomnia, reproductive issues and mild depression. This increase of symptoms has been linked to synthetic chemicals and petrochemicals in our environment.

Synthetic offshoots from plants or essential oils? Here are just 2 examples of many: we've cured cold symptoms for generations with Vicks Vaporub, whose main ingredients are synthetic forms of mint (menthol), laurel tree (camphor), and eucalyptus (eucalyptol), in addition to cedar leaf, nutmeg and pine oils. Coca Cola was originally marketed as a 'nerve tonic,' containing various essential oils of citrus and spices.

However, essential oils cannot be trademarked, patented or controlled, and big pharma has little interest in pursuing something without monetary benefit. They do copy, mimic or try to reproduce synthetic versions of some essential oils, like the aforementioned Vick's Vaporub. But working with pure essential oils? No.

As far as clinical studies, from the 1980s to 1990s, there were more and more exciting studies of essential oils and their effects on chronic, metabolic and hormonal diseases. Then in 2001, there was a sudden stop in research – Dr. Schnaubelt in his book "The Healing Intelligence of Essential Oils" (2011) says "It does not appear outlandish to suspect reservations on the part of corporate pharmacology about remedies that may be too cheap and too accessible." (16)

It is also possible the fallacy developed or existed that antibiotics were wiping out diseases for good, and new research or development wasn't needed? In any case, there was a slow-down of studies.

Yet, new discoveries were made in the later 20th century, such as helichrysum essential oil able to mediate tissue protective and regenerative quality by going after free radicals; common essential oils were shown as effective agents to prevent osteoporosis, by Muhlbauer, Lozano, Palacio, Reinli and Felix; Dr. Anne-Marie Giraud-Robert's long-term studies have shown various essential oils are effective in treatment of hepatitis B and C.

Inhibit HMG CoA Reductase is a key enzyme in humans and plants. Essential oils can inhibit this enzyme and the synthesis of cholesterol which in turn is relevant for the prevention or the inhibition of carcinogensis and tumor growth shows. (17) Research has demonstrated that tumor cells can be shut off by essential oils.

"The intimate connection of essential oils to the evolution of enzymes in our bodies is but one factor that demonstrates how essential oils have naturally, from time immemorial, interfaced with humans." says Dr. Schnaubelt in "The Healing Intelligence of Plants." (18)

SUMMARY

Looking at the chain of history, Romans got their knowledge of essential oils from the Greeks, who had gotten their knowledge from the Egyptians, who had gotten it from Sumeria and Babylonia. Europeans of the 18th century learned of essential oils from the 17th, and they from the 16th and on back. There was a "death period" in the Dark Ages, but nevertheless, through trade, wars and travels, the knowledge found a way back from the east to the west, and has survived. Now today, we are re-discovering, learning and taking the knowledge to new applications and potential modalities. These may include life-saving approaches to the antibiotic-resistant bacterial problems, and a more natural way to deal with many common ailments (without side effects.)

REFERENCES

1) Rolf Deininger, "The Magic World of Essential Oils and Scents, Their Influence on the Psyche. Wholistic Aromatherapy, A Scientific Conference on Therapeutic Uses of Essential Oils. 1995.

2) Lawless J., Aromatherapy and the Mind. 1994.

3) p 86, Gattefossé's Aromatherapy, 1937.)

4) http://www.woundsresearch.com/article/8088

5) Ayurveda, 2015.

6) Gloria McBreen

7) http://www.suzannebovenizer.com/aromatherapy-essential-oils/history

8) http://www.bbc.com/news/uk-england-nottinghamshire-32117815

9) http://www.encyclopedia.com/topic/Philippus_Aureolus_Paracelsus.aspx

10) http://tisserandinstitute.org/infographic-essential-oils-as-antimicrobials/

11) (Nicholas Culpeper, The English Physician, 1653. online through Yale Medical Library: http://www.med.yale.edu/library/historical/culpeper/culpeper.htm)

12) http://www.jonnsaromatherapy.com/history2.html

13) Gattefosse book or else Tisserand's book.

14) Bio/Tech News, 2014.

15) Steinman & Epstein, 1995

16) Schnaubelt, Dr. Kurt. The Healing Intelligence of Essential Oils. 2011.

17) IBID page 26

18) IBID

Acknowledgements

I thank my great husband, Harlan, who is always supportive!

Kathy Heshelow

BIBLIOGRAPHY

Balz, Rodolphe. The Healing Power of Essential Oils. Lotus Light. 1996.

Butje, Andrea. Essential Living: Aromatherapy Recipes for Health & Home. 2nd edition. 2015.

Dodt, Colleen. The Essential Oils Book. Storey Communications, 1996.

Gattefossé, Rene-Maurice. Aromatherapy. Translated by Robert B. Tisserand. Saffron Walden, 1993.

Guenther, Ernest. The Essential Oils – Vol 1: History – Origin in Plants – Production – Analysis. D. Van Nostrand Company, 1948.

Harding, Jennie. The Essential Oils Handbook. Watkins Publishing London. 2008.

Johnson, Dr. Scott A. Evidence-Based Essential Oil Therapy. Scott A. Johnson Professional Writing Services, LLC , 2015

Johnson, Dr. Scott A. Surviving When Modern Medicine Fails. Scott A. Johnson Professional Writing Services, LLC. 2014.

Johnson, Dr. Scott A. and Plant, Dr. Joshua. Synergy, It's an Essential Oil Thing: Revealing the Science of Essential Oil Synergy with Cells, Genes and Human Health. 2015.

Lawless, Julia. The Illustrated Encyclopedia of Essential Oils. Thorsons, 1995.

Schnaubelt, Dr. Kurt. Advanced Aromatherapy. Healing Arts Press, 1998.

Schnaubelt, Dr. Kurt. The Healing Intelligence of Essential Oils. Healing Arts Press, 2011.

Schnaubelt, Dr. Kurt. Medical Aromatherapy. Frog, Ltd. 1999.

Schnaubelt, Dr. Kurt (Editor). Unlimited Possibilities: Proceedings of the 8th International Aromatherapy Conference. Nov 2015.

Stewart, Dr. David. Healing Oils of the Bible. Care Press. 2014.

Stewart, Dr. David. Quantum Physics, Essential Oils and the Mind-Body Connection (brochure). Sound Concepts, 2008.

Tisserand, Robert B. The Art of Aromatherapy. Healing Arts Press. 1977

Tisserand, Robert B. and Young, Rodney. Essential Oil Safety: A Guide for Healthcare Professionals. 2nd edition. Churchill Livingstone.

Wildwood, Chrissie. The Encyclopedia of Aromatherapy. Healing Arts Press, 2000.

Worwood, Valerie Ann. The Complete Book of Essential Oils & Aromatherapy. New World Library. 1991.

Worwood, Valerie Ann. The Fragrant Mind: Aromatherapy for Personality, Mind, Mood and Emotion. New World Library. 1996.

Printed in Poland
by Amazon Fulfillment
Poland Sp. z o.o., Wrocław